YOUR KNOWLEDGE HAS VALUE

- We will publish your bachelor's and
  master's thesis, essays and papers

- Your own eBook and book -
  sold worldwide in all relevant shops

- Earn money with each sale

Upload your text at www.GRIN.com
and publish for free

Sania Nayab, Sadia Anwar, Samina Sagheer

Challenges of Implementation of Agile In Distributed Environment

GRIN Publishing

Bibliographic information published by the German National Library:

The German National Library lists this publication in the National Bibliography; detailed bibliographic data are available on the Internet at http://dnb.dnb.de .

Imprint:

Copyright © 2014 GRIN Verlag GmbH
Print and binding: Books on Demand GmbH, Norderstedt Germany
ISBN: 978-3-656-86657-2

This book at GRIN:

http://www.grin.com/en/e-book/286438/challenges-of-implementation-of-agile-in-distributed-environment

GRIN - Your knowledge has value

Since its foundation in 1998, GRIN has specialized in publishing academic texts by students, college teachers and other academics as e-book and printed book. The website www.grin.com is an ideal platform for presenting term papers, final papers, scientific essays, dissertations and specialist books.

Visit us on the internet:

http://www.grin.com/

http://www.facebook.com/grincom

http://www.twitter.com/grin_com

Challenges of Implementation of Agile In Distributed Environment

Sadia Anwar	Samina Sagheer	Sania Nayab
UAF	UAF	UAF
Pakistan	Pakistan	Pakistan

Abstract

Previous research has focused on both challenges and opportunities with increased distance in distributed software development. Interestingly most opportunities are found on customer level in large business organizations where most challenges are introduced at the level of development practice. Distance has been recognized as major challenge to the use of agile methods. In this paper, we are trying to fulfill the upcoming demands for managing major challenges of agile in distributed environment.

Keywords:

Agile in distributed environment, Agile team dynamics, Customer communication challenges, Coordination among team members, Time distances in agile

1:Introduction

The world around us has changed. Everything seems to happen faster and more unexpected than before. There is dramatically more uncertainty and change out there, and it started long before the financial crisis. There will be more change in the future. Companies are shifting from mass production orientation to knowledge intensive organizations where the human capital is the most valued asset. Companies need to realize that their people are actually highly competent and mature, and expect to be empowered, appreciated, and well - treated as adults. People both want and can take responsibility. In this new environment, we need to respond faster and think differently about what best motivates and drives great performance in organizations. [1]

Distributed software development and global sharing of information and resources have become a common business reality. Moreover, the changing business needs force organizations to develop and evolve new software systems at internet speeds. Distributed software development typically relies on formal mechanisms such as detailed architectural design and plans to address barriers to team communication that result from geographical separation. Distributed software development is establishing itself as a commonplace approach in software development. Despite the opportunities, distributed development also presents a host of challenges, and the research community has not yet developed a thorough understanding of these challenges or how they can be overcome. [2]

Agile software development is a group of software development methods based on iterative and incremental development, where requirements and solutions evolve through collaboration between self-organizing, cross-functional teams. It promotes adaptive planning, evolutionary development and delivery, a time-boxed iterative approach, and encourages rapid and flexible response to change. It is a conceptual framework that promotes foreseen tight iterations throughout the development cycle. [3]

Unlike plan based process methods, agile methods deal with unpredictability by trusting on people and creative efforts instead of formalized processes (Cockburn, A. (2002).). Agile methods are totally value based whereas most plan based methods are not clear in their underlying philosophy; agile methods are focused by their devotion to a set of agile values. (Lindstrom, L. and Jeffries, R. (2004)).

But due to the globalization of many organizations distributed collaborations and virtual teams have become increasingly common, distributed development projects are needed for this purpose consisting of teams working together to achieve project goals from different geographic locations. (Sarker, S., and Sahay, S. (2004).

As a result of these major trends, software development organizations have been determined to blend agile software development methods like XP (eXtreme Programming) and distributed development to gather the benefits of both. There may be certain challenges that may arise from blending agility with distributed development. [4]

The careful incorporation of agility in distributed software development environments is essential in addressing several challenges to communication, control and trust across distributed teams. This paper demonstrates that how a balance between agile and distributed approaches can help to meet these challenges. Performance of teams and companies in distributed environments should also be measured somehow and companies are seeking good matrices how to do that. We want to extend the study to observe real settings and report the outcome that how these two approaches will meet the challenges in the near future.

2: Material and Methodology

2.1 Challenges in Agile Distributed Development/Environment:

Communication Challenges
As agile development relies more on informal interactions than overt documentation, it creates a real challenge in a distributed environment. Effective communication is considered vital in software development, and is emphasized in agile and distributed development environments. Communication improved record of communication between geographical temporal distance and reduce opportunities for synchronous communication. Communication provides potential for stimulating innovation and sharing best practice. [5]

Lack of Control
Lack of control emphasizes poor focus and controlling ability across distributed teams. Following points are considered due importance:
People- vs. process-oriented control. In distributed development environments, control is often achieved by establishing formal processes. Agile environments, on the other hand, are more people-oriented and control is established through informal processes.

Fixed vs. evolving quality requirements. Due to the limited ability to control activities of remotely located teams, distributed development often relies on fixed, upfront commitments on quality requirements. In contrast, agile development relies on ongoing negotiations between the developer and the customer for determining the acceptable levels of quality at various stages of development.

Lack of Trust
It focuses poor bounding among team members of agile which creates a biggest challenge for development in distributed environment. It creates lack of team moral.
Formal vs. informal agreement. Contracts in agile environments are loosely and informally defined. In contrast, distributed development relies on explicit targets, milestones, and detailed specification of requirements.
Lack of team cohesion. In distributed development, participants at different sites are less likely to perceive themselves as part of the same team when compared to co-located participants. Lack of cohesiveness and shared view of goals are problems in such an environment. These problems are even more pronounced in agile development, which emphasizes constant cooperation on all aspects of the project. [4]

Distance Directions
Temporal distance
Temporal distance is a measure of the displacement in time faced by two actors' wishes to interact. It reduced opportunities for synchronous communication.

Geographical distance
It is the measure of the force required one actor to see and other actor. It increases cost and material of managing face to face meetings.

Sociocultural distance
Sociocultural distance is the measure of an actor understands about other actors' ethics and moral practices.

Efficient communications one of the most essential factor in development and is more important even both in agile and distributed environments.

Organizations following distributed agile development should focus on establishing and efficient customer relation enabling more impressive communication links. However, the possible contradiction between the traditional and agile approaches may have an effect on customer communications.

Approaching the usefulness of a development approach is rigorous and requires more experimental. Thus, we claim that the customer relationship and organization politics that bound information sharing may lead any communication medium to become incompetent. Instead of highlighting on choosing and appropriate communication challenge, the organizations should first concentrate on making an efficient customer relationship and environment that enables effective communication. [2]

Project teams involved in agile distributed development must adopt all the prescribed practices that address questions of organizations in context of customer's needs.

3: Tables and Findings

Challenges in Distributed Development		Features of Agile Development	Latest disputes in Agile Distributed Development
Communication challenges	.Difficult to initiate communication •Misunderstanding/miscommunication • Dramatically decreased frequency of communication • Increased communication cost— time, money, and staff • Time difference	.Lack of formal communication • Increased demand for informal communication	Communication need vs. communication impedance

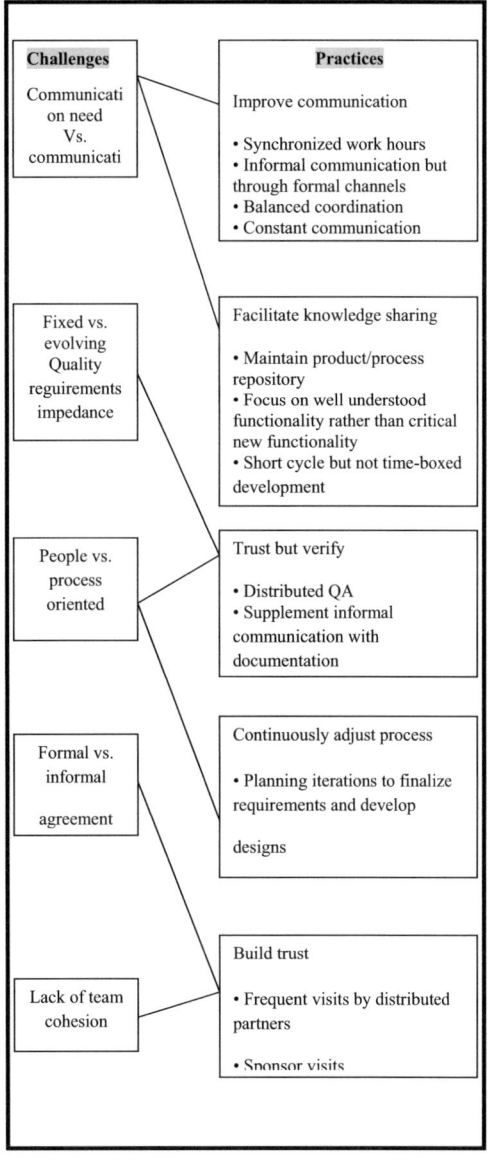

| Lack of control | Difficult to control process and quality across distributed teams | .Lightweight process • Ongoing negotiation • Reliance on skilled people | Fixed vs. evolving quality requirements People vs. process oriented control |
| Lack of trust | • Lack of trust between distributed team members • Lack of team morale | • Cohesive team • Trust built progressively •Short commitment | Formal vs. informal agreement Lack of team cohesion |

Table 1 Mapping between

The practices to achieve distribution may be characterized as agile but disciplined have evolved in the organizations after focusing repeatedly on common issues of these organizations. These practices are in the spirit of light weight process methods, but have been streamlined to cover the marketing demands of distributed development as well.

By continuously adjusting the process instead of hardly following the agile development practices as commonly described, the companies continuously squeeze them to adjust according to the changing requirements of their projects.

Conclusion

Global software development opens new opportunities, there is little doubt that it presents new challenges and this research fully described the challenges of agile implementation in distributed environment. It also explores how agile practices can reduce three kinds of distance that are temporal, geographical and sociocultural in global software development. These practices mentioned in this article are found to be useful for reducing communication, coordination.

References:

i. Bjarte Bogsnes (2009). Beyond Budgeting in a Lean and Agile World…, LNBIP 31, pp. 5–7.

ii. Mikko K., Minna P., and Kieran C. (2009) Distributed Agile Development: A Case Study of Customer Communication Challenges, LNBIP 31, pp. 161–167.

iii. A decade of agile methodologies: Towards explaining agile software development. The Journal of Systems and Software 85 (2012) 1213– 1221

iv. Balasubramaniam R., Lan. C., Kannan M., *and* Peng X. (2006) Can distributed software development be agile?, COMMUNICATIONS OF THE ACM October 2006/Vol. 49, No. 10

v. H. Holmström, B. Fitzgerald, P. J. Ågerfalk, and Conchúir. O. E., (2006) agile practices reduce distance in global software development, Information system Management, vol 23, No. 3, pp.7-18.

vi. Cockburn, A. (2002). *Agile Softwar Development* Boston: Addison-Wesley.

vii. Lindstrom, L. and Jeffries, R. (2004) Extreme Programming and Agile Software Development Methodologies, *Information Systems Management,* 24(3), pp. 41–60.

viii. Sarker, S., and Sahay, S. (2004). Implications of space and time for distributed work: an interpretive study of US-Norwegian systems development teams, *European Journal of Information Systems,* 13, pp. 3–20.